I0766295

Erika Figula - Ferenc Margitics - Zsuzsa Pauwlik

The Bully
Background Factors of School Bullying Behaviour

The Bully /Background Factors of School Bullying Behaviour/

Authored by: Erika Figula PhD., Ferenc Margitics PhD., Zsuzsa Pauwlik PhD.
(figula.erika@nye.hu)
Edited and published by: Ervin K. Kery
(editor@kery.org)

ISBN: 9781706199847

PREFACE

Our research group established by the Department of Psychology at the College of Nyíregyháza investigates the phenomena of school bullying and harassment. The term 'school bullying covers the behaviour where the aggressive act has no obvious cause (non-reactive aggression).

Our research focuses on the question that among upper school primary school students and high school students what kind of background factors may stand in the background of aggressive attitude and behavior patterns of school bullying (bully, victim, bystander, intervener participant and helper participant). During our research, we charted those background factors, which help to understand the process of the development of bully, victim, participant and bystander behavior patterns, as well as they allow the development of the options of efficient mental hygiene.

In this book we examined the relation between bully behavior pattern in school bullying and certain parental treatments (such as; parental solicitude, parental overprotection and parental restriction). We wanted to find an answer to the question: what kind of temperament and character traits the students have, who become bullies through school bullying and what their typical emotional reactions are.

In our research we used the following instruments: the Questionnaire on School Bullying, the Hungarian adaptation of Goch's Family Socializational, the Hungarian adaptation of the Parental Bonding Instrument, the Hungarian version of Cloninger's Temperament and Character Inventory, the Hungarian version of Differential Emotions Scale, The Hungarian version of Weismann's Scale of Dysfunctional Attitudes and The Hungarian adaptation of the Folkman–Lazarus Conflict Solving Questionnaire.

INTRODUCTION

According to his results, Olweus (1993) divides up bullies into two groups: active aggressors and passive aggressors. Active aggressors are the initiatives of school bullying.

They are those students, who harass directly. There are some students, who are the harassers' friends and they take part because of courage in the harassment but at the same time they are devoured by fear too because they do not want to become victims. They are named sympathizers by the literature.

According to Olweus (1993) active aggressors fancy themselves. They are neither shy nor uncertain. On the contrary, they have too much confidence. Active aggressors are often older and stronger than their victims, which is likely increasing their self-assessment.

Therefore, they consider themselves tough, dominant, hearty. The demonstration of power and the domination over others' fate are their typical characteristics.

Typical active aggressors have great need

for power and control therefore they appear to be rude and unfriendly (Busch, 1998.).

According to Korte (1999), in general, active aggressors show less empathy with their victims and they do not feel guilty.

According to Ziegler and Ziegler (1997), active aggressors are impulsive, excitable, and inflammable and they have low frustration tolerance, the smallest provocation may cause escalated reaction in the students, it can be a glance, a gesture or simply someone was in the wrong place, at the wrong time.

Kassis (2003) concluded that bullies are not only more frequently violent, but more often deploy social violence.

Margitics et al. (2010) demonstrated that those students with antisocial temperament may become victims through school bullying, who can be characterized by high novelty seeking, low harm-avoidance and reward dependence. Seeking danger, defiant confrontation, non-conformism, rigidity are typical of this temperament type. So they do not become victims of school bullying. If they did not initiate violence, they will be always ready to become intervener participants and they do not remain bystanders.

Contrary to Olweus (1993), Kassis (2003) believes that active aggressors judge themselves negatively, they do not accept themselves and they are not optimistic about their future. In point of basic cognitive and emotional behaviors (such as talent, confidence, tendency to depression and emotional control), the scored results were unstable.

According to Kassis' interpretation (2003), these results show that the students, who are particularly uncertain, tend to become aggressors because of their anger and frustration.

Dambach (2002) also believes that insults, failures and frustrations cause fear and anger in many active aggressors and force them to hurt the weaker ones, which brings them momentary relief.

Examining the connection between the behavior patterns of school bullying and the character types, Margitics et al. (2010) found that the melancholic character type, who is characterized by low self-directness, cooperativeness, self-transcendence experience, tends to become victim or bully through school bullying.

This character type lives through a few positive emotions; his/her emotions are mainly characterized by suffering, shame and hatred. In case of school bullying, beside melancholic character types, paranoid character types might also become bullies, who can be characterized by high self-directedness, self-transcendence and low cooperativeness.

This character type is characterized by low cooperativeness ability; he or she is suspicious, tenacious, and goal-oriented. If they are not bullies, they do not remain bystanders; they tend to become intervener participants.

According to Kathleen (2007), we need to see the typology of bullies more differentiatedly than active and passive bullies because there can be differences between the confident bullies and the unconfident bullies (who reflect on their actions after doing it). But perhaps uncertain aggressors mean the status of sympathizers and followers.

According to Rost (1998), bullies show themselves strong and confident but inside they feel fear.

METHODOLOGY

Participants

Factors of Family Socialization

In the study 647 (301 girls, 346 boys) primary and high school students took part. The distribution of the sample according to schools was the following:

> Primary school, upper school: 293 participants (140 girls, 150 boys)
> High school: 354 participants (161 girls, 193 boys)

The sample according to age:

> Primary school, upper school: 13,2 year old
> High school: 16,7 year old

Temperament and Character

The data for the research project were gathered from students of secondary grammar schools.

341 students participated in the project,

195 women and 146 men.

The average age was 16,4 years (standard deviation: 1,4).

Emotions, Attitudes and Coping Mechanisms

The data for the research project were gathered from students of primary education at elementary schools and secondary grammar schools.

706 students participated in the project, 397 women and 309 men.

The average age was 15,2 years (standard deviation: 1,7).

Measures

Factors of Family Socialization

We applied two different questionnaires.

The Hungarian adaptation of Goch's Family Socializational Questionnaire (Goch, 1998, Sallay & Dabert, 2002).

The questionnaire describes the following dimensions of family socialization:

> - type of the family atmosphere (rule-oriented family atmosphere, conflict-oriented family atmosphere),
> - breeding target (breeding for autonomy, autonomy as a target of breeding, breeding for conformity, conformity as a breeding target),
> - educational attitudes (consistent educational attitude, manipulative educational attitude, inconsistent educational attitude)
> - educational style (supporting educational style, punishing educational style).

The Hungarian adaptation of the Parental Bonding Instrument (Tóth & Gervai, 1999).

The questionnaire has three main scales: love and care, overprotection, and restriction, applied separately to the mother and the father.

Temperament and Character

The Hungarian version of Cloninger's Temperament and Character Inventory (Rózsa et al. 2005)

The main scales of the measure describe four temperament and three character dimensions:

> ➤ The temperament-scales are novelty seeking, harm avoidance, reward dependence, persistence

> ➤ The character-scales are self-directedness, cooperativeness, self-transcendence.

Emotions

Hungarian version of Differentional Emotions Scale (Oláh, 2005).

Izard (1971) developed Differentional Emotions Scale in order to differentiate between the basic emotions. The inventory is suitable for examining the ability of experiencing certain basic emotions as a permanent characteristic feature.

With the help of a frequency scale it examines how often the basic emotions appear.

Differential Emotions Scale consists of a scale identifying ten basic emotions. The questionnaire describes the following fundamental emotions:

> ➤ Trait of Interest
> ➤ Trait of Enjoyment
> ➤ Trait of Surprise
> ➤ Trait of Distress
> ➤ Trait of Anger
> ➤ Trait of Disgust
> ➤ Trait of Contempt
> ➤ Trait of Fear
> ➤ Trait of Shame
> ➤ Trait of Guilt
> ➤ Trait of Anxiety

The Hungarian adaptation of the questionnaire was done by Oláh (2005), who found the reliability of the scales good (Cronbach-alpha=0,49-0,76).

Attitudes

The Hungarian version of Weismann's Scale of Dysfunctional Attitudes (Weisman & Beck, 1979, Kopp, 1994).

The scale included question of following attitudes:

> desire for external appraisal, need for affections, performance orientation, perfectionism, rightful and intensive requirements towards the environment, omnipotence (intensive altruism) and external control - autonomy.

Coping Mechanisms

The Hungarian adaptation of the Folkman–Lazarus Conflict Solving Questionnaire (Kopp, 1994).

The questionnaire contains 22 items and is used to reveal the behaviour of individuals in difficult situations. Respondents use a four-grade scale for each answer, from "entirely irrelevant" to "fully relevant."

Folkman and Lazarus arranged conflict-solving strategies into problem-based and emotion-based categories. The surveys conducted by Kopp and Skrabski (1995) confirmed the validity of this categorization. They found three problem-driven, three emotion-driven and one support-seeking factor. These are the following:

> Problem analysis
> Cognitive restructuring
> Conformance
> Emotion-driven action
> Seeking emotional balance
> Retrieval
> Call for help
> A summary indicator of the problem-driven coping strategy
> A summary indicator of the emotion-driven coping strategy

Problem-driven coping strategies (problem analysis, cognitive re-structuring, conformance) measure the ability of the individual to analyse the problem, to influence the reasons and to obtain control over it. It also measures the ability of cognitive re-structuring.

The second three emotion-driven coping strategies (emotion-driven action, seeking emotional equilibrium, retrieval) and call for help will come forward when the individual is not satisfactorily familiar with the problem or feels unable to obtain control over the situation.

The Examination of School Bullying

The Questionnaire on School Bullying (Figula et al., 2019).

For purposes of identifying patterns of behaviour in school bullying, the School Bullying Questionnaire was used.

The 70 items of SBQ offers options of "almost never," "sometimes," "often," "almost always," and investigates the phenomena of school bullying and abuse in everyday life through five dimensions.

With the exception of "intervener participant" scale, all dimensions include further subscales. (Chart 1).

The Criteria of Compiling the Research Group and the Control Group

When we formed the test groups, we considered the results scored on the scales of Questionnaire on School Bullying, which examines the behavior patterns of school bullying, within this, which quartiles the tested people got into.

Chart 1. Scales and Subscales of the School Bullying Questionnaire

Scales and Subscales	Item	Cronbach-alfa
Victim Scale	**33**	**0,847**
Cognitive Subscale (Conscious recognition of abuse and processing it)	15	0,877
Affective Subscale (The emotional effect of abuse)	12	0,864
Somatic reaction (Somatic reaction to abuse / acting out)	3	0,758
Lack of Social Support Subscale (Lack of acceptance in class community)	3	0,814
Intervener Participant Scale	**3**	**0,784**
Helper Intervener Scale	**8**	**0,753**
Intervening to Pacify Subscale	3	0,748
Intervening to Ask for Help Subscale	2	0,778
Affective Subscale (Inner tension as a result of witnessing aggression)	3	0,749
Bystander Scale	**9**	**0,768**
Keeping Distance Subscale	6	0,758
Fear Subscale	3	0,743
Bully Scale	**17**	**0,843**

Physical Aggression Subscale	4	0,845
Verbal Aggression Subscale	5	0,849
Exclusion Subscale	5	0,754
Advantage From Attack Subscale	3	0,768

RESULTS

Factors of Family Socialization

The structure of Family Socialization factors

With the help of second-rate factor analysis (varimax rotation) we examined the patterns of parental educational dimensions, its underlying structure (during the study- according to general practice- not less than 0,4 (factor gravity) rotated factors were taken into account (Chart 2).

Chart 2. Second Rate Factor Analysis for the Dimensions of Parental Nurturing (l>0.4)

Dimensions of Parental Bonding	Factor 1	Factor 2	Factor 3	Factor 4
Rule oriented family atmosphere r	0,641			
Conflict oriented family atmosphere		0,730		
Manipulative educational		0,670		

attitude			
Inconsistent educational attitude		0,758	
Consistent educational attitude	0,662		
Punishing educational style	0,772		
Supportive educational style			-0,469
Breeding for conformity	0,759		
Breeding for autonomy			-0,619
Maternal affection-care		-0,595	
Paternal affection-care		-0,648	
Maternal overprotection				0,854
Paternal overprotection				0,878
Maternal restriction			0,898	
Paternal restriction			0,895	

The analysis arranged parental educational dimension into four factors, which together explained 64,9% of the variance.

The first factor, which explains 25,2% of the variance, demonstrates rule oriented family atmosphere, which is characterized by conformity as parental educational goal and it associates with punishing educational style and consistent educational attitude.

The second factor, which explains 21,4% of the variance, demonstrates conflict oriented family atmosphere, which is characterized by conflict oriented family atmosphere, the manipulative and inconsistent educational attitude of the parents and the lack of love and care.

The third factor, which explains 10,6% of the variance, demonstrates restrictional parental treatment, which is characterized by the lack of parental support and breeding for autonomy

The fourth factor, which explains 7,7%of the variance, describes parental overprotection.

The connection between bully behavior patterns of school bullying and parental educational effects were revealed by linear regression analysis (stepwise method: dependant variable was the behavior patterns of school bullying, parental educational effects were used as predictor).

Chart 3 shows the results of linear regression analysis in case of bully behavior pattern.

Chart 3. Interrelationship between Parental Rearing Effects with the Behaviour Patterns of the Bully (approved models; p<0.05)

Predictor	B	t	P<
Women: $F_{totál}$=17,119; df=3/301; p<0,000			
Maternal affection-care	-0,197	-3,364	0,001
Rule oriented family atmosphere	0,173	3,191	0,002
Maternal overprotection	0,144	2,268	0,024
Men: $F_{totál}$=19,510; df=3/346; p<0,000			
Conflict oriented family atmosphere	0,238	3,956	0,000
Maternal overprotection	0,199	3,122	0,001
Paternal affection-care	-0,175	-3,089	0,007

In case of the girls, bully behavior pattern, from the parental educational effects, showed a significant, negative connection with maternal affection-care and a positive one with maternal overprotection and rule oriented family atmosphere, which together explained 12,4% of the variance of bully behavior pattern.

In case of the boys, bully behavior pattern, from the parental educational effects, showed a significant, positive connection with conflict oriented family atmosphere, maternal overprotection and a negative one with paternal affection-care, which together explained 18,7% of the variance of bully behavior pattern.

Temperament and Character

We examined what differences exist between the test groups (bully vs. not bully) on the basis of the results scored on the Bully Scale of the Questionnaire on School Bullying examining the behavior patterns of school bullying.

Figure 1 shows the averages scored on the certain scales of Temperament and Character Inventory of bully vs. not bully control groups in case of the girls.

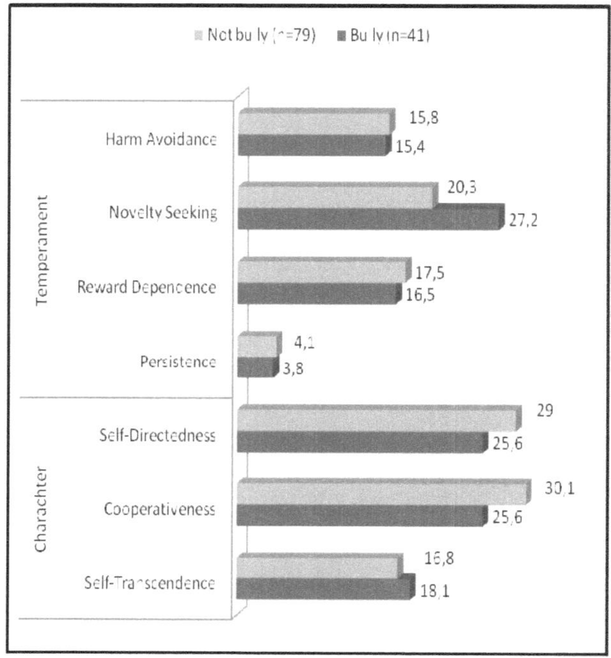

Figure 1. Averages Achieved on the Individual Scales of the Temperament and Character Inventory by Bully Test Group vs. Non-Bully Test Group (girls)

In case of the girls, on the basis of Comparative Statistical Analysis, we found significant differences in point of temperament traits, only in case of novelty seeking, in point of character traits, in case of cooperativeness and self-directedness between the test groups.

We found novelty seeking more typical of the girls becoming bullies of school bullying (t=6,149, p<0,001), cooperativeness and self-directedness were more typical of the girls not becoming bullies (t=3,676, p<0,01).

Figure 2 shows the averages scored on the certain scales of Temperament and Character Inventory of bully vs. not bully control groups in case of the boys.

In case of the boys, on the basis of Comparative Statistical Analysis, we found significant differences in point of temperament traits, in case of novelty seeking and reward dependence, in point of character traits, in case of cooperativeness and self-directedness between the bully vs. not bully test groups.

We found novelty seeking (t=3,646, p<0,01) and reward dependence(t=3,621, p<0,01), more typical of the boys becoming bullies of school bullying, cooperativeness (t=4,837, p<0,001) and self-directedness (t=3,145, p<0,05) were more typical of the boys not becoming bullies.

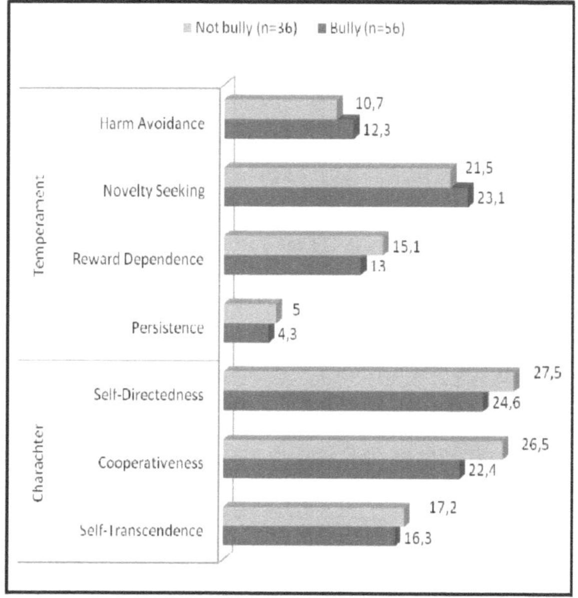

Figure 2. Averages Achieved on the Individual Scales of the Temperament and Character Inventory by Bully Test Group vs. Non-Bully Test Group (boys)

The connection between bully behavior pattern of school bullying and temperament and character traits were revealed by linear regression analysis (stepwise method: dependant variable was the behavior patterns of school bullying, independent variables were the certain temperament and character traits and their constituent personality traits.

Chart 4. shows the results of linear regression analysis in case of bully behavior pattern.

Chart 4. Correlation between Temperament and Character Features and the Behaviour Pattern of the Bully (approved models; p<0.05)

Predictor	B	t	P<
Women: $F_{totál}$=17,144; df=4/195; p<0,000			
Novelty seeking	0,257	3,889	0,000
Social acceptance	-0,262	-3,942	0,000
Transpersonal identity	-0,165	-2,588	0,010
Empathy	-0,176	-2,559	0,011
Men: $F_{totál}$=21,438; df=3/146; p<0,000			
Novelty seeking	0,315	3,459	0,000
Cooperativeness	-0,308	-3,018	0,000
Transpersonal identity	-0,158	-2,006	0,046

In case of the girls, bully behavior pattern, from the temperament an character traits and their constituent personality traits, showed a significant, negative connection with social acceptance, transpersonal identity, empathy and a positive one with novelty seeking, which together explained 26,5 % of the variance of bully behavior pattern.

In case of the boys, bully behavior pattern, from the temperament an character traits and their constituent personality traits, showed a significant, negative connection with cooperativeness, transpersonal identity and a positive one with novelty seeking, which together explained 12,5 % of the variance of bully behavior pattern.

Emotions

We examined what difference exists between the test groups in point of basic emotions on the basis of the results scored on the scales of the bully behavior pattern' Questionnaire on School Bullying.

Figure 3 shows the averages scored on the certain scales of Differential Emotions Scale of bully vs. not bully control groups in case of the girls.

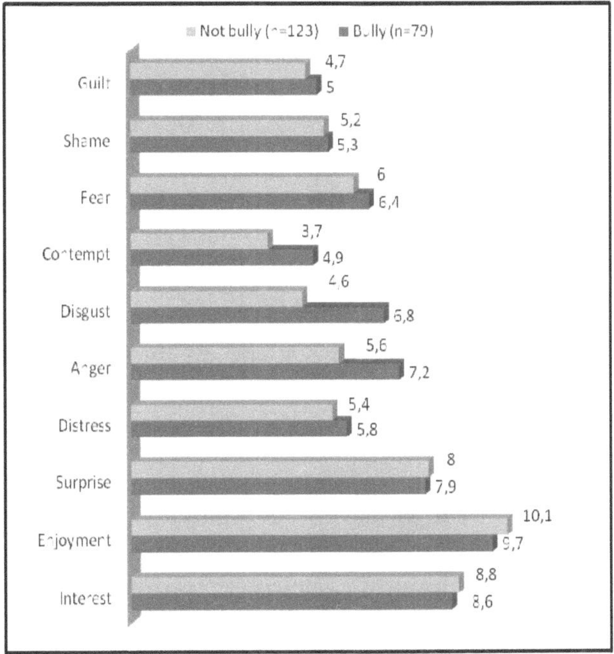

Figure 3. Averages Achieved on the Individual Scales of the Differentional Emotions Scale by Bully Test Group vs. Non-Bully Test Group (girls)

Comparative Statistical Analysis shows that there were significant differences between the test groups in point of more basic emotions.

These are the following:

> ➢ Disgust (t=7,615, p<0,000)
> ➢ Anger (t=6,290, p<0,000)
> ➢ Contempt (t=4,827, p<0,000)

These results indicate that disgust, anger contempt were rather typical of the girls becoming bully of school bullying than the girls not becoming bully.

Figure 4 shows the averages scored on the certain scales of Differential Emotions Scale of bully vs. not bully test groups in case of the boys.

Comparative Statistical Analysis shows that there were significant differences between the test groups in point of more basic emotions.

These are the following:

> ➢ Contempt (t=5,107, p<0,00)
> ➢ Anger (t=5,056, p<0,000)
> ➢ Disgust (t=4,975, p<0,000)

These results indicate that contempt, anger and disgust were rather typical of the boys becoming bully of school bullying than the boys not becoming bully.

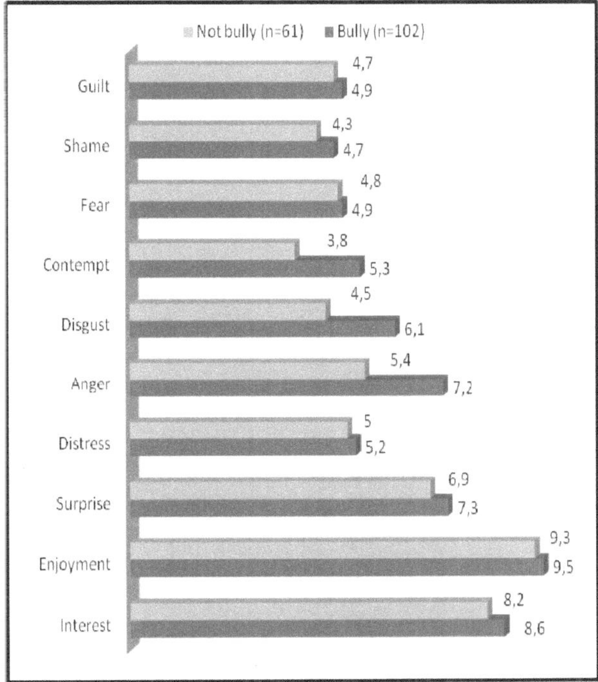

Figure 4. Averages Achieved on the Individual Scales of the Differential Emotions Scale by Bully Test Group vs. Non-Bully Test Group (boys)

The connection between the bully behavior pattern of school bullying and the basic emotions were revealed by linear regression analysis (stepwise method: dependant variable was bully behavior pattern, basic emotions were used as predictors).

Chart 5 shows the regression analysis of the basic emotions according to the components of bully behavior pattern

Chart 5. Relationship of Fundamental Emotions with the Behaviour Pattern of the Bully (approved models; p<0.05)

Predictor	B	t	P<
Women: $F_{totál}$=30,739; df=2/397; p<0,000			
Disgust	0,292	5,387	0,000
Anger	0,120	2,206	0,028
Men: $F_{totál}$=20,566; df=4/309; p<0,000			
Anger	0,227	3,757	0,000
Guilt	-0,190	-3,619	0,000
Disgust	0,211	3,228	0,001
Contempt	0,156	2,339	0,007

In case of the girls, bully behavior pattern, from the basic emotions, showed a significant, positive connection with disgust and anger, which together explained 13,5 % of the variance.

In case of the boys, bully behavior pattern, from the basic emotions, showed a significant, positive connection with also disgust, anger as well as contempt and a negative one with guilt, which together explained 21,3 % of the variance.

These results indicate that the students becoming bullies of school bullying – without reference to gender differences- feel anger and disgust, which associates with contempt and lack of guilt in case of the boys.

We also examined that what the connection is between the certain components of bully behavior pattern (physical aggression, verbal aggression, exclusion, positive profit (benefit of the assault)) and the basic emotions (linear regression, stepwise method: dependant variable is the components of bully behavior pattern, basic emotions were used as predictors).

Chart 6 shows the revealed connections with this method.

In case of the girls, the physical aggression component of bully behavior pattern, from the basic emotions, showed a significant, positive connection with disgust and anger, which together explained 5,7 % of the variance.

In case of the boys, the physical aggression component of bully behavior pattern, from the basic emotions, showed a significant, positive connection with anger and a negative one with guilt, which together explained 11,1 % of the variance..

Chart 6. Regression Analysis of Fundamental Emotions versus the Individual Components of the Bully Behaviour Pattern (approved models; p<0.05)

Predictor	B	t	P<
Physical aggression			
Women: $F_{totál}$=9,520; df=2/397; p<0,000			
Anger	0,221	4,221	0,000
Disgust	0,130	2,407	0,013
Men: $F_{totál}$=19,046; df=2/309; p<0,000			
Anger	0,318	5,785	0,000
Guilt	-0,180	-3,271	0,001
Verbal aggression			
Women: $F_{totál}$=38,832; df=1/397; p<0,000			
Disgust	0,299	6,232	0,000
Men: $F_{totál}$=19,591; df=3/309; p<0,000			
Anger	0,278	4,482	0,000
Guilt	-0,181	-3,339	0,001
Disgust	0,182	2,913	0,004
Exclusion			
Women: $F_{totál}$=34,123; df=1/397; p<0,000			
Disgust	0,282	5,841	0,000
Men: $F_{totál}$=17,348; df=2/309; p<0,000			
Contempt	0,188	3,101	0,002
Disgust	0,186	3,069	0,002

Positive profit (benefit of the assault)			
Women: $F_{totál}$=9,987; df=3/397; p<0,000			
Anger	0,149	2,840	0,005
Contempt	0,143	2,729	0,007
Shame	-0,126	-2,578	0,010
Men: $F_{totál}$=16,961; df=2/309; p<0,000			
Disgust	0,266	4,253	0,000
Anger	0,235	4,281	0,000
Contempt	0,234	3,809	0,000

In case of the girls, the verbal aggression component of bully behavior pattern, from the basic emotions, showed a significant, positive connection with disgust, which together explained 9 % of the variance.

In case of the boys, the verbal aggression component of bully behavior pattern, from the basic emotions, showed a significant, positive connection with anger and disgust and a negative one with guilt, which together explained 16,2 % of the variance.

In case of the girls, the exclusion component of bully behavior pattern, from the basic emotions, showed a significant, positive connection with disgust, which together explained 8 % of the variance.

In case of the boys, the exclusion component of bully behavior pattern, from the basic emotions, showed a significant, positive connection with disgust as well as contempt, which together explained 10,2 % of the variance.

In case of the girls, the positive profit component of bully behavior pattern, from the basic emotions, showed a significant, positive connection with anger and contempt and a negative one with shame, which together explained 7,1 % of the variance.

In case of the boys, the positive profit component of bully behavior pattern, from the basic emotions, showed a significant, positive connection with disgust, anger and contempt, which together explained 18,1 % of the variance.

Attitudes

We examined what difference exists between the test groups in point of dysfunctional attitudes on the basis of the results scored on the bully scale of the behavior patterns' Questionnaire on School Bullying.

Figure 5 shows the averages scored on the certain scales of Scale of Dysfunctional Attitudes of bully vs. not bully test groups in case of the girls.

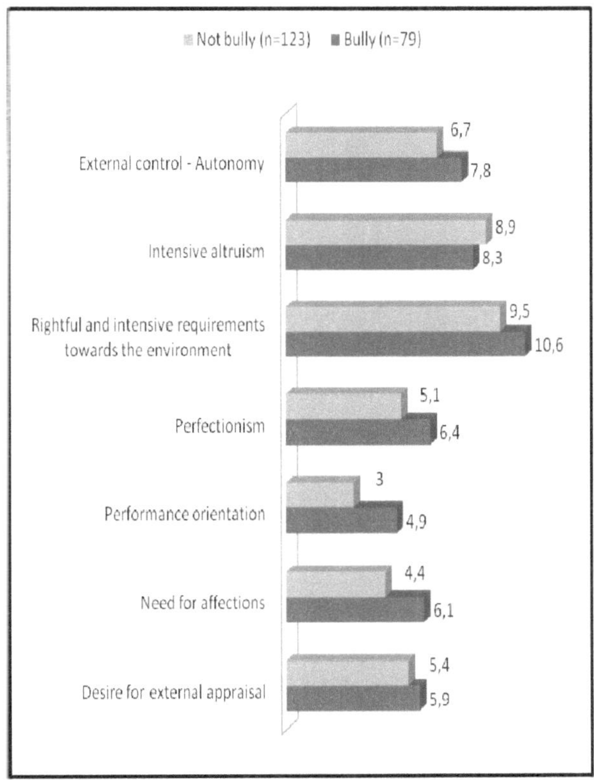

Figure 5. Averages Achieved on the Scale of Dysfunctional Attitudes by the Bully Test Group vs. Non-Bully Test Group (girls)

Comparative Statistical Analysis (two-sample t-test) shows that there were significant differences between the test groups in point of more dysfunctional attitudes.

These are the following:

➤ Performance orientation (t=2,940, p<0,004)
➤ Need for affections (t=2,636, p<0,009)
➤ Perfectionism (t=2,453, p<0,015)
➤ External control - Autonomy (t=2,345, p<0,020)
➤ Rightful and intensive requirements towards the environment (t=2,042, p<0,042)

These results indicate that performance orientation, need for affections, perfectionism, external control and intensive requirements towards the environment were rather typical of the girls becoming bullies of school bullying than the girls not becoming bullies.

Figure 6 shows the averages scored on the certain scales of Scale of Dysfunctional Attitudes of bully vs. not bully test groups in case of the boys.

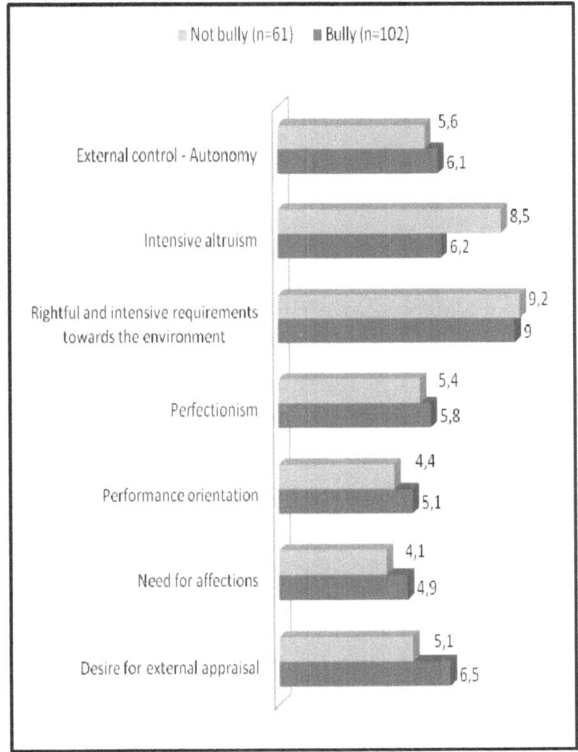

Figure 6. Averages Achieved on the Scale of Dysfunctional Attitudes by the Bully Test Group vs. Non-Bully Test Group (boys)

Comparative Statistical Analysis (two-sample t-test) shows that there were significant differences between the test groups in point of only two dysfunctional attitudes.

These are the following:

> Intensive altruism (t=3,876, p<0,000)
> Desire for external appraisal (t=2,978, p<0,005)

These results indicate that desire for external appraisal was rather typical of the boys becoming bullies of school bullying than the boys not becoming bullies, as well as altruism was not typical of bullies.

The connection between the bully behavior pattern of school bullying and the dysfunctional attitudes was revealed by linear regression analysis (stepwise method: dependant variable was the certain behavior patterns, dysfunctional attitudes were used as predictors).

Chart 7 shows the results of linear regression analysis in case of bully behavior pattern.

In case of the girls, bully behavior pattern, from the dysfunctional attitudes, showed a significant, positive connection only with performance orientation, which together explained 2,4 % of the variance.

Chart 7. Correlation between the Attitudes that Might Become Dysfunctional with the Bully Behaviour Pattern (approved models; p<0.05)

Predictor	B	t	P<
Women: $F_{totál}$=9,585; df=1/397; p<0,002			
Performance orientation	0,154	3,096	0,002
Men: $F_{totál}$=11,034; df=2/309; p<0,000			
Intensive altruism	-262	-4,435	0,000
Performance orientation	0,180	3,035	0,003

In case of the boys, bully behavior pattern, from the dysfunctional attitudes, showed a significant, positive connection also with performance orientation and a negative one with intensive altruism, which together explained 6,7 % of the variance of bully behavior pattern.

We also examined that what the connection is between the certain components of bully behavior pattern (physical aggression, verbal aggression, exclusion, positive profit (benefit of the assault)) and the dysfunctional attitudes (linear regression, stepwise method:

dependant variable is the components of bully behavior pattern, dysfunctional attitudes were used as predictors).

Chart 8 shows the revealed connections with this method.

Chart 8. Regression Analysis of the Attitudes that Might Become Dysfunctional Versus the Individual Components of the Bully Behaviour Pattern (approved models; p<0.05)

Predictor	B	t	P<
Physical aggression			
Women: $F_{totál}$=7,689; df=1/397; p<0,006			
Need for affections	0,138	2,771	0,006
Men: $F_{totál}$=6,165; df=2/309; p<0,002			
Performance orientation	0,176	2,925	0,004
Intensive altruism	-0,172	-2,862	0,004
Exclusion			
Women: $F_{totál}$=9,289; df=2/397; p<0,000			
Performance orientation	0,209	4,024	0,000
Intensive altruism	-0,144	-2,763	0,006
Men: $F_{totál}$=10,749; df=1/309; p<0,000			
Intensive altruism	-0,216	-3,881	0,000
Positive profit (benefit of the assault)			
Women: $F_{totál}$=6,367; df=1/397; p<0,012			
Performance orientation	0,126	2,523	0,012

Men: $F_{totál}=7{,}445$; $df=2/309$; $p<0{,}001$			
Intensive altruism	-0,227	-3,708	0,000
Desire for external appraisal	0,154	2,506	0,013

In case of the girls and the boys, the physical aggression component of bully behavior pattern did not show significant, positive connection with any of the dysfunctional attitudes.

In case of the girls, the verbal aggression component of bully behavior pattern, from the dysfunctional attitudes, showed a significant, positive connection only with need for affections, which explained 1,9% of the variance.

In case of the boys, the verbal aggression component of bully behavior pattern, from the dysfunctional attitudes, showed a significant, positive connection with performance orientation and a negative one with intensive altruism, which explained 3,9% of the variance.

In case of the girls, the exclusion component of bully behavior pattern, from the dysfunctional attitudes, showed a significant, positive connection with performance orientation and a negative one with intensive altruism, which explained

4,5 % of the variance.

In case of the boys, the exclusion component of bully behavior pattern, from the dysfunctional attitudes, showed a significant, negative connection only with intensive altruism, which explained 4,7 % of the variance.

In case of the girls, the positive profit component of bully behavior pattern, from the dysfunctional attitudes, showed a significant, positive connection with performance orientation, which explained 4,9 % of the variance.

In case of the boys, the positive profit component of bully behavior pattern, from the dysfunctional attitudes, showed a significant, positive connection with desire for external appraisal and a negative one with intensive altruism, which explained 4,6 % of the variance.

Coping Mechanisms

We examined what differences exist between the test groups in point of coping strategies on the basis of the results scored on the bully scale of the behavior patterns' Questionnaire on School Bullying

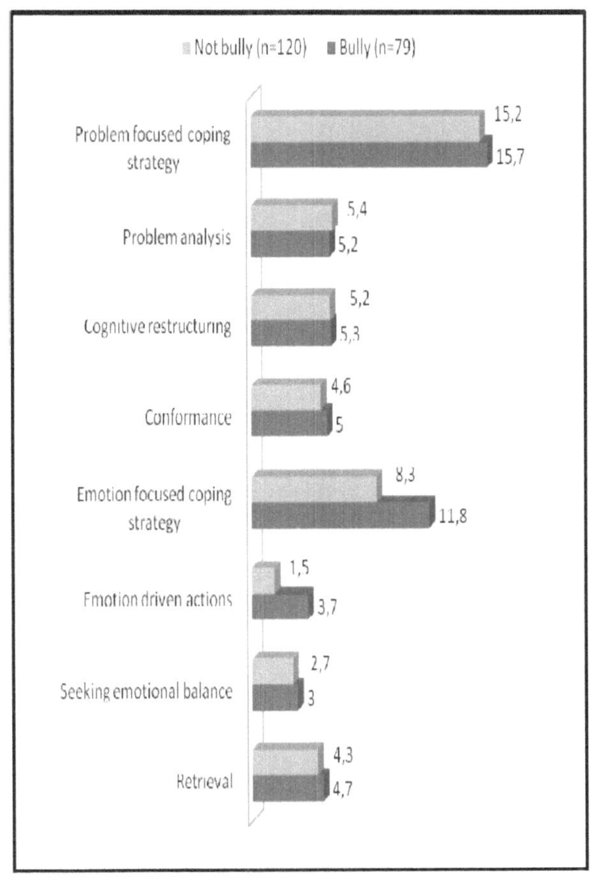

Figure. 7 Achieved on the Individual Scales of the Conflict Solving Inventory by the Bully Test Group vs. Non-Bully Test group (girls)

Figure 7 shows the averages scored on the certain scales of Conflict Solving Inventory of bully vs. not bully test groups in case of the girls.

Comparative Statistical Analysis shows that there were significant differences between the test groups in point of only two coping strategies.

These are the following:

- Emotion driven actions (t=7,118, p<0,000)
- Emotion focused coping strategy (t=5,003, p<0,000)

These results indicate that the emotion focused coping strategies especially emotion driven actions were rather typical of the girls becoming bullies of school bullying.

Figure 8 shows the averages scored on the certain scales of Conflict Solving Inventory of bully vs. not bully test groups in case of the boys.

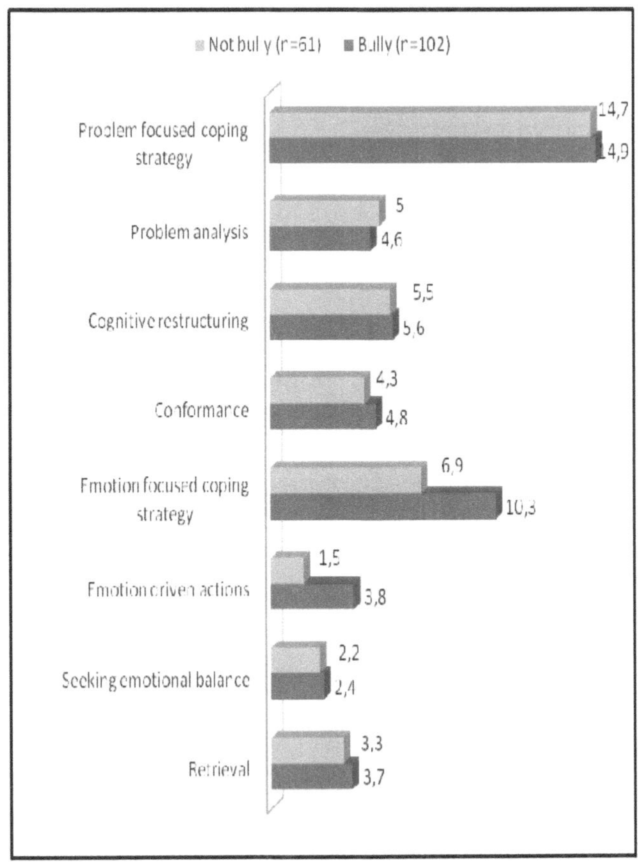

Figure 8. Averages Achieved on the Individual Scales of the Conflict Solving Inventory by the Bully Test Group vs. Non-Bully Test group (boys)

Comparative Statistical Analysis shows that there were significant differences between the test groups in point of only two coping strategies.

These are the following:

> Emotion driven actions (t=6,246, p<0,000)
> Emotion focused coping strategy (t=4,301, p<0,000)

These results indicate that the emotion focused coping strategies especially emotion driven actions were rather typical of the boys becoming bullies of school bullying.

The connection between the bully behavior pattern of school bullying and the coping strategies was revealed by linear regression analysis (stepwise method: dependant variable was the bully behavior pattern, coping strategies were used as predictors).

Chart 9 shows the results of linear regression analysis in case of victim behavior pattern.

In case of the girls, bully behavior pattern, from the coping strategies, showed a significant, positive connection only with emotion driven actions, which explained 13,4 % of the variance.

Chart 9. Correlation of Conflict Solving Strategies with the Bully Behaviour Pattern (approved models; p<0.05)

Predictor	B	t	P<
Women: $F_{totál}$=60,986; df=1/397; p<0,000			
Emotion driven actions	0,366	7,809	0,000
Men: $F_{totál}$=52,578; df=2/309; p<0,000			
Emotion driven actions	0,507	10,202	0,000
Problem analysis	-0,111	-2,240	0,024

In case of the boys, bully behavior pattern, from the coping strategies, showed a significant, positive connection also with emotion driven actions and a negative one with problem analysis, which explained 25,6 % of the variance of bully behavior pattern.

We also examined that what the connection is between the certain components of bully behavior pattern (physical aggression, verbal aggression, exclusion and positive profit (benefit of the assault)) and the coping strategies (linear regression, stepwise method: dependant variable is the components of bully behavior pattern, coping strategies were used as predictors).

Chart 10 shows the revealed connections with this method.

Chart 10 Regression Analysis of Conflict Solving Strategies Versus the Individual Components of the Bully Behaviour Pattern (approved models; p<0.05)

Predictor	B	t	P<
Physical aggression			
Women: $F_{totál}$=15,869; df=2/397; p<0,000			
Emotion driven actions	0,271	5,510	0,000
Seeking emotional balance	-0,105	-2,139	0,033
Men: $F_{totál}$=86,441; df=1/309; p<0,000			
Emotion driven actions	0,469	9,297	0,000
Verbal aggression			
Women: $F_{totál}$=44,046; df=1/397; p<0,000			
Emotion driven actions	0,317	6,637	0,000
Men: $F_{totál}$=70,815; df=1/309; p<0,000			
Emotion driven actions	0,433	8,415	0,000
Exclusion			
Women: $F_{totál}$=25,876; df=1/397; p<0,000			

Emotion driven actions	0,248	5,087	0,000
Men: $F_{tot\acute{a}l}$=12,832; df=1/309; p<0,000			
Emotion driven actions	0,200	3,582	0,000
Positive profit (benefit of the assault)			
Women: $F_{tot\acute{a}l}$=13,339; df=1/397; p<0,000			
Seeking emotional balance	0,181	3,652	0,000
Men: $F_{tot\acute{a}l}$=60,836; df=1/309; p<0,000			
Emotion driven actions	0,407	7,800	0,000

In case of the girls, the physical aggression component of bully behavior pattern, from the coping strategies, showed a significant, positive connection with emotion driven actions and a negative one with seeking emotional balance, which together explained 7,5 % of the variance.

In case of the boys, the physical aggression component of bully behavior pattern, from the coping strategies, showed a significant, positive connection only with emotion driven actions, which explained 22 % of the variance.

In case of the girls, the verbal aggression component of bully behavior pattern, from the coping strategies, showed a significant, positive connection only with emotion driven actions, which explained 10

% of the variance.

In case of the boys, the verbal aggression component of bully behavior pattern, from the coping strategies, showed a significant, positive connection only with emotion driven actions, which explained 18,7 % of the variance.

In case of the girls, the exclusion component of bully behavior pattern, from the coping strategies, showed a significant, positive connection only with emotion driven actions, which explained 6,1 % of the variance.

In case of the boys, the exclusion component of bully behavior pattern, from the coping strategies, showed a significant, positive connection only with emotion driven actions, which explained 4 % of the variance.

In case of the girls, the positive profit component of bully behavior pattern, from the coping strategies, showed a significant, positive connection only with seeking emotional balance, which explained 5,1 % of the variance.

In case of the boys, the positive profit component of bully behavior pattern, from the coping strategies, showed a significant, positive connection only with emotion driven actions, which explained 18,5 % of the variance.

DISCUSSION

Factors of Family Socialization

Researches on bullying show that, there is a connection between family atmosphere and aggressive behavior. It is likely that those children who find aggressive behavior useful it is typical of them that conflict is often present in their family, they take part in bullying at home and in aggressive behavior, and they feel that aggression has a functional value to achieve their goals. Surely they learn these behaviors at home and it is likely that the learned things at home are practiced at school by them (Espelage & Swearer, 2003).

The role of family in the development of bullying has been examined by several researches. Researchers have found strong links among the aggressive behavior of young people and the lack of family cohesion (Gorman-Smith et al., 1996), inadequate family control (Farrington, 1991), family bullying (Thornberry, 1994), belligerence (Loeber & Dishion, 1983) and poor problem-solving skills (Tolan et al., 1986).

Furthermore, the presence of family

conflicts and parental problems also show close contact with aggression in childhood (Henggeler et al, 1998).

More researchers have revealed connection among parental educational style, family atmosphere and school bullying. For example, according to Olweus' Scandinavian Youth Research (1980, 1993) he concluded that the violent boys' families can be often characterized by the lack of coziness, the use of physical bullying within the family and the inability to control extra-curricular activities.

The above findings in Bowers, Smith, Binney's research (1994) were confirmed and supplemented by that the harassers' family members have high claim to power. About the families of the victims it turned out that the family is very cohesive and probably the mother is overprotective (Berdondini & Smith, 1996).

In point of family socialization background effects, our research results show that parental overprotection –without reference to gender differences- may cause the appearance of the victim behavior pattern of school bullying, from the components of which , maternal overprotection is typical of the girls, maternal and paternal overprotection are typical of both the girls and the boys.

The connection among the further parental educational effects is different between the boys and the girls. In case of the boys, bully behavior pattern is present in a conflict oriented family atmosphere. Within this, the effect of conflict oriented family atmosphere and the lack of maternal love and care is strong, which associates with manipulative and inconsistent educational attitudes.

In case of the girls, parental love and care especially lack of maternal love and care was in close contact with bully behavior pattern. In case of the girls, the appearance of bully behavior pattern can be caused by rule oriented family atmosphere; in case of the boys, it can be caused by consistent educational attitudes.

Temperament and Character

In Cloninger's (1987) integrative personality model importance is attached equally to biological and genetic factors, as well as learning and social impacts with respect to the development of personality. While congenital elements play a principal role in the evolution of temperament factors, learning and environment have the main effect on character factors.

Temperament is characterized by varied automatic responses to emotional stimuli, while the feature of the character is determined by the conception of the self, of others and the world.

Despite the fact that differences that are manifested in temperament factors may be observed already in early infanthood, the evolution of character takes place as the socialization proceeds, through the social impacts to which the individual is exposed. Temperament and character together determine the entire personality.

Cloninger's temperament- and character model is arguably the most comprehensive and elaborate of today's personality theories, taking into consideration the effects of the biological and environmental factors influencing the development of the personality. In this model it is possible to examine healthy and psycho-pathological personalities within the same standardized system and concept, including the discussion of the reasons behind, and the procedures going on in the background of, certain psychological phenomena.

In Cloninger's model, a mature, fully developed personality's competetent situation and problem-solving abilities and attitudes are always in control, overriding the innate characteristic features of the individual and those received from the parents of the individual in the early years of life. In the case of a high level of self-directedness, we talk about a conscious shaping of our behaviour. In addition to this, a mature personality is also characterised by a low level of harm-avoidance.

Examining the temperament and character traits, we found that novelty seeking temperament trait and lack of cooperativeness, self-detachment character traits can be in the background of becoming bullies (without reference to gender differences).

Those people, who seek novelty, are impulsive, like to discover new things, excitable and can be easily provoked to fight or escape. If these temperament traits associates with the lack of cooperativeness (social intolerance, vindictiveness, lack of interest in other people) and controlling behavior (self-detachment) then it is likely that the students become bullies through school bullying.

We found that novelty seeking was the most typical temperament trait of the girls. Their most typical character traits were social intolerance, vindictiveness and self-detachment. Novelty seeking was also the most typical temperament trait of the boys becoming bullies. Lack of cooperativeness and self-detachment were also their most typical character traits.

These results confirm Ziegler and Ziegler's (1997) results, who found that the bullies are impulsive, excitable and inflammable, which is connection with novelty seeking temperament trait.

Korte's research results (1999) can be explained by the lack of cooperativeness, according to which, in general, active aggressors show less empathy with their victims and they do not feel guilty.

Emotions, Attitudes and Coping Mechanisms

Our research results, which examine emotions, attitudes and coping, show that the boys, who become bullies through school bullying –without reference to gender differences-primarily, feel anger and disgust, which force them to do emotion driven actions.

They deduct anger in an aggressive way towards their peers. Their performance orientation can be increased.

Beside the above mentioned emotions: anger, disgust, contempt as well as guilt and intensive altruism are also typical of the boys becoming victims. In case of them, emotion driven actions associate with the lack of problem analysis.

REFERENCES

Berdondini, L., Smith, P.K. (1996): Cohesion and power in the families of children involved in bully/victim problems at school: An Italian replication. *Journal of Family Therapy, 18,* 99-102.

Bowers, K., Smith, P. K., Binney, V. (1994): Perceived family relationships og bullies, victims, and bully/victims in middle childhood. *Journal of Social and Personal Relationships, 11,* 215-232.

Busch, L. (1998). *Aggression in der Schule. Präventionsorientierte und differentielle Analyse von Bedingungsfaktoren aggressiven Schülerverhaltens.* Inaugural-Dissertation. Wettenberg: Selbstverlag.

Cloninger, C. R. (1987): A systematic method for clinical description and classification of personality variants. *Arch. Gen. Psychiatry. 44,* 573-588.

Dambach, K. E. (2003). Mobbing unter Kindern und Jugendlichen Unsere Jugend. *Die Zeitschrift für Studium und Praxis der Sozialpädagogik,* **55.** 3. sz. 507– 516.

Espelage, D. L., Swearer, S. M. (2003): Research on School Bullying and

Victimization: What Have We Learned and Where Do We Go From Here? *School Psychology Review. 32,* 365-383.

Goch, I. (1998). *Entwicklung der Ungewissheitstoleranz. Die Bedeutung der familialen Socialization.* Regensburg: Roderer.

Farrington, D. P. (1991): Childhood aggression and adult violence: Early precursors and later-life outcomes. In D. J. Pepler, K. H. Rubin (Eds.) *The development and treatment of childhood aggression.* Hilsdale, NJ: Erlbaum, 5-29.

Figula E, Margitics F, Pauwlik Zs. (2019): *The Questionnaire on School Bullying /handbook/.* KeryPub. New York.

Gorman-Smith, D., Tolan P. H., Zelli, A. & Huessmann, L. R. (1996): The relation of family functioning to violence among inner-city minority youth. *Journal of Family Psychology, 10,* 115-129.

Henggeler, S. W., Schoenwald, S. K, Bourdin, C. M., Rowland, M. D., Cunningham, P. B. (1998): *Multisystemic treatment of anti social behavior in children and adolescents.* New York, The Guilford Press.

Izard, C.E. (1971): *The Face of Emotions.* Appleton-Century-Crofts, New York.

Kassis, W. (2003). *Wie kommt die Gewalt in die Jungen? Soziale und personale Faktoren der Gewaltentwicklung bei männlichen Jugendlichen im Schulkontext.* Bern, Stuttgart, Wien: Haupt Verlag.

Kathleen, R. (2007): *Bullying auf dem Schulweg: Das Schulbus-Phänomen. Erstellung eines Persönlichkeitsprofils von Tätern und Opfern. Eine empirische Studie in Thüringen. Dissertation zur Erlangung des academischen Grades doctor philosophiae* (Dr. phil.), Friedrich Schiller Universität Jena, 2007.

Kopp, M. (1994). *Orvosi pszichológia.* Budapest: SOTE Magatartástudományi Intézet.

Korte, J. (1999). *Faustrecht auf dem Schulhof. Über den Umgang mit aggressiven Verhalten in der Schule.* Weinheim, Basel: Beltz Verlag.

Loeber, R., Dishion, T. (1983): Early predictors of male delinquency: A review. *Psychological Bulletin, 94,* 68-99.

Margitics, F; Figula, E; Pauwlik, Zs (2010): *Temperamentum, karakter és iskolai erőszak.* Nyíregyháza, Élmény '94 Bt.142 p.

Oláh, A. (2005): *Érzelmek, megküzdés és*

optimális élmény. Trefor Kiadó, Budapest.

Olweus D. (1980): Familian and temperamental determinants of agressive behavior in adolescent boys: a causal analysis. *Developmental Psychology,* 16. 23-35.

Olweus, D. (1993): Bully/victim problems among school children: Long-term consequences and an effective intervention program. In S. Hodhings (Ed.), *Mental disorder and crime,* (pp. 317- 349). Thousand Oaks, CA: Sage Publications.

Rost, D. (1998). *Handbuch Pädagogische Psychologie.* Weinheim: Beltz Verlag.

Rózsa S., and Kállai, J., and Osváth, A., and Bánki M. Cs. (2005). *Temperamentum és karakter: Cloninger pszichobiológiai modellje. A Cloninger-féle temperamentum és karakter kérdőív felhasználói kézikönyve.* Budapest: Medicina Könyvkiadó Rt.

Sallay, H., and Dabert, C. (2002). Women's perception of parenting: a German-Hungarian comparison. *Applied Psychology in Hungary, 3-4,* 55-56.

Thornberry, T. P. (1994): *Violent families and youth violence* (Office of Juvenile

Justice and Deliquency Prevention Fact Sheet No. 21). Washington, DC: Department of Justice.

Tolan, P. H., Cromwell, R. E., Braswell, M. (1986): The application of family therapy to juvenile delinquency: A critical review of the literature. *Family process, 15,* 619-649.

Tóth, I., and Gervai, J. (1999). Szülői Bánásmód Kérdőív (H-PBI): a Parental Bonding Instrument magyar változata. *Magyar Pszichológiai Szemle, 54,* 551-566.

Weisman, A.N., and Beck, A.T. (1979). *The Dysfunctional Attitude Scale.* Thesis, University of Pennsylvania.

Ziegler, R. Ziegler, A. (1997). *Gewalt in der (Grund) Schule. Analysen und pädagogische Konsequenzen.* Aachen: Shaker Verlag.

PREVIOUS PUBLICATIONS

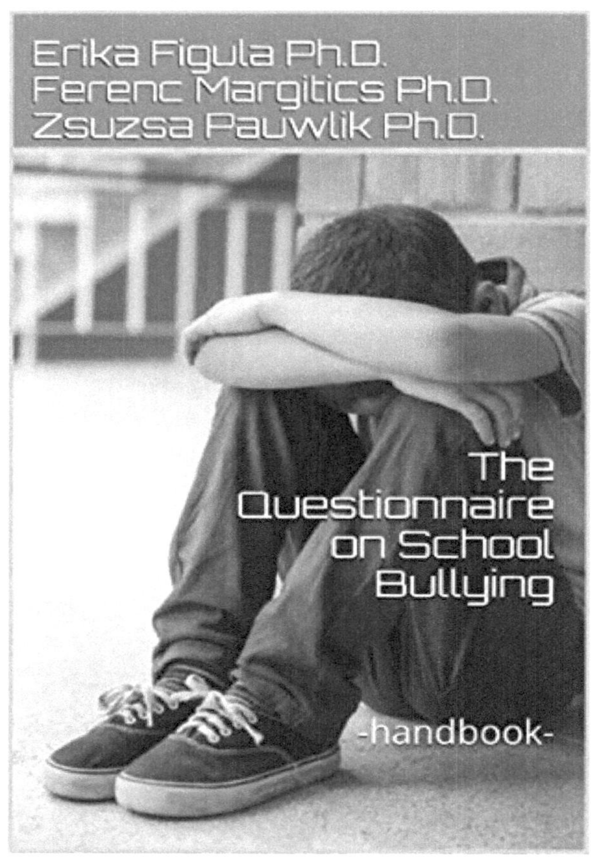

Look inside at Amazon.com
https://www.amazon.com/dp/B07XD2S48T

Look inside at Amazon.com

https://www.amazon.com/dp/B07YYNN4K2